Selling in the
Bear Woods

Twelve Disciplines Good Sales People Must Master to Become Great!

by

Bob Robert Mann
&
Bryan Townsend

Bob Robert Mann & Bryan Townsend
Talladega, Alabama

Library of Congress Catalog Card Number: 97-91291

ISBN: 0-9661848-0-7

Printed in the United States of America

This book is dedicated to:

Roy E. Mann

*Role model, loving father, best friend, and sales mentor
to Bob Robert Mann*

&

Jimmy E. Woodard

Sales mentor to Bryan Townsend

Acknowledgments

The authors would like to thank:

Sandra Mann and Judy Townsend for their patience; Phillip Van Hooser, Judy Marston, Marolyn Fields, and Dalton Lott for their encouragement; Ralph Hood for his contributions, assistance in editing and wonderful foreword which illustrates his writing ability far surpasses ours; Mike Fralix for his advice and suggestions; Gary Adair for his assistance in editing; and Judy Townsend and Julie Tran for editing and proofreading.

Foreword

This sales book is different. In the first place, the authors themselves are different.

I have been selling things for over fifty years, since I first went into business as a pre-schooler, selling garden supplies door-to-door. (Business was brisk, but short lived. The supplies belonged to my father, I was selling them below his cost and without his knowledge, and my business suffered a precipitous cessation once he discovered the source of my ill gotten gains.) Later, I legitimately sold everything from tomatoes to airplanes, and am the proud owner of a file folder full of certificates proclaiming me to be salesman of the week, and month, and the winner of this or that sales contest.

So, I am no stranger to selling. But I stand in awe of the authors, Bob Robert Mann and Bryan Townsend, and have for many years.

Bryan Townsend was earning a handsome sum of money selling when he was only twenty-five. He sold in a small local market, to the same people every month. It takes a real pro--an ethical pro--to make it in a small market, and if he had never left that market Bryan's sales career would be remarkable. About ten years ago, however, I watched Bryan jump from that local market to a national market--from chasing rabbits, as the book says, to hunting bears. He did it rapidly, thoroughly, professionally and ethically, and is today a national leader in that field.

Bob Robert Mann's sales career is equally impressive. Bob was selling in a regional market when I first met him in the eighties, and doing it well. He, too, could have remained in that arena forever, making a substantial income as a well-respected and much trusted professional. But he, like Bryan, wanted more. I remember worrying about him when he set out to hunt big bears in the big woods. It was a wasted effort on my part. Since then, I have watched Bob become not just a *great* bear hunter, but a *legendary* bear hunter, doing things that I and others knew were not difficult, but *impossible*.

We readers are fortunate that Bryan and Bob are not just great salespeople, but also great teachers and great story tellers. This book tells exactly how they hunt bear in the big woods, and how you can, too.

But be forewarned--neither Bryan nor Bob claim to know any secret to *easy* sales success. Instead they know--and provide in this book--numerous tools which, when applied vigorously, consistency, and ethically, are almost guaranteed to yield success in the long run. Selling has been described as the highest paid hard work and lowest paid easy work. Bryan and Bob are both highly paid.

Note that so far I have used the term *ethical* or *trusted* four different times in describing Bryan and Bob. Between them, they don't own an ounce of sleaze. This book won't teach you how to fool, dupe or overcome the customer. Instead, you will learn how to reach sales success by *helping* the customer.

For the salesperson who wants to do it right, this is a wonderful book. Read, enjoy, and prosper.

Ralph Hood, CSP
Professional Speaker & Author

Contents

Bears Hunt Back

Y ou have to walk softly in the bear woods, because bears will *hunt you*! It's much easier and safer to chase rabbits. However, mother nature and the free enterprise system reward both skill and risk. Those who are skilled enough to handle greater risk, earn greater rewards. Those who are adept at chasing rabbits become more valuable when they learn to hunt bear.

A great salesperson, loaded with a handful of selling skills and sales credentials, can earn a handsome income selling almost anything. From this point, increasing income requires either a bigger territory or bigger game. Time and space limit the number of calls one individual can make, so there is a finite limit to how much territory you can handle because you can only help a certain number of clients solve a certain number of problems. Bigger game, consequently, is the better option, but going after bigger game always requires solving bigger problems and taking greater risks.

There is always the risk of failure. Bigger accounts come with more sophisticated buyers and more complicated demands on sellers, and hunting in the bear woods means competing with tougher competitors who will always come after you. Then, there is the risk of losing bigger accounts once you've established yourself in a bigger league. The big league buyers in the bear woods are even less loyal than minor league buyers, and think nothing of shutting down a few factories before lunch. Bears are much more vicious than rabbits.

Since you are reading this book, it's obvious you are thinking about selling more and doing better. Perhaps you realize *good* salespeople are abundant, but *great* sales professionals are not. You want to be counted among the few and you are already tempted to enter the bear woods, even if you haven't thought about it in that light. Pilgrims beware! Bears bite. But, with proper training, you can learn to catch them before they catch you. This book can be your guide.

The purpose of this book is to help you grow to the next level. We want it to be of value to you by helping you adopt the culture of a sales champion.

You will find the following core beliefs essential to your quest:

✦ **Customers are those who benefit from whatever you do when you say you are working.**

✦ **All customers want, and have a right to expect, value.**

✦ **Service means making it easy for customers to get what they need from you.**

✦ **Value is the work product of good service.**

✦ **You must always exceed customer expectations.**

✦ **Profit is earned by finding or creating solutions which are more valuable to your customers than they cost you to provide.**

This book will also serve as your encourager. If you are already a remarkable sales pro, and you are willing to prepare yourself to hunt bigger game, you can make it happen, but you *must* prepare! You must not only be willing, you must take action, to increase your level of knowledge and to discipline yourself to master even the little things--*every detail*. The little things become the big things from here on out. Little mistakes are costly in the bear woods. It takes the very finest grinding to make a sharp blade salient. Honing your craft means adopting a new culture where it is crucially important to make a big deal over the little things.

There is little new under the sun in terms of the dynamics of human relationships, and there is nothing new in selling. The craft is as old as commerce itself, and the first cave man to sell the first wheel to the first prospect was faced with the same question as the sales person who sold the latest computer yesterday: *"What's this thing going to do for me?"*

Yours is the ultimate *people* profession. You live in a world of people, not a world of things. Things change. People do too, but not very much. Just a little change on your part is going to make a big difference!

In these pages you will find a number of skills or characteristics identified. You will be familiar with all of them. Now is the time to start thinking of them as *disciplines* to be *mastered* so you can sell more effectively with greater confidence and move up to the next level in your high and noble craft.

High and noble? Oh, yes! Without sales people like you, ours would be a feudal economy. Without deal makers like us to move goods and services, millions of people would be out of work, without food, shelter or access to medical benefits because, as you know, *nothing happens until something is sold.*

A Word of Caution

Being good often keeps sales people from becoming *great.* In sales, the respect and rewards that come from just being good often make many people comfortable and complacent. Maybe you don't want to become one of the great ones. If not, it's most unlikely that you will. More than anything else, greatness requires desire.

Getting the initial sale is the easiest and simplest part of a long term sales partnership. Continuing to remain a value can be tough. Moving up in sales means raising the bar. Once you do that, people will consistently expect more from you. On a daily basis, you'll have to rise to meet the new standards.

Of course there is an upside to this. If it was easy, there would be legions of *master-track* sales people and the rewards of the endeavor would be greatly diminished.

A good salesman we know once ventured into the bear woods. On his first call, he went through the mechanics, gave details of the item, market support, pricing, advertising, and closed with his tried and true magic words, *"This is a great product, fabulous pricing, and has a super effective marketing support program."*

The buyer glared at him and responded, *"My boy, we don't buy any junk in this office--those are just the minimum standards for getting an item viewed here."*

In the bear woods, everything is bigger, better, faster, quicker, and more costly. You will not only have to do more to be successful here, you will have to do all the fundamentals better. All standards will be higher. This book will help prepare you for the expedition.

Billy Bob Baker
Hits the Big Time

Once, Bob Baker served on a jury. On the first ballot, his was the lone vote for the plaintiff in a count of eleven to one. Three and a half hours later, the foreman delivered a unanimous verdict to the judge, on behalf of the plaintiff! Bob had persuaded eleven other jurors to change their vote. His conviction and perseverance persuaded the others to come over to his side. He could sell slide rules to Hewlett-Packard.

As an advertising salesman for a local newspaper, Bob did very well selling ads to "Mom and Pop" stores and local chain outlets. His talent was rewarded with promotions and after just a few years in the industry, he found himself selling to some impressive regional accounts. Life was good.

Most would have been satisfied with the level of success Bob had achieved. He had a comfortable home, a condo at the beach, two cars, a new pick up truck, and a very nice boat. He had mortgages, but they were manageable. His bills were paid and he had some handsome investments.

But, Bob was not motivated by money alone; most top sales people are not. Top performers in sales are unique individuals who live for the chase. Like horses that run for roses, or kids on video games who get addicted to wild sounds and bright flashes as the screen totals up worthless points, sales champions are most often motivated by challenge.

Bob was perfectly happy selling to "Mom and Pop", until he peaked out. He needed a bigger mountain. After you have *been there & done that,* those who have what it takes to be a top performer in sales, get bored and have to move on to bigger challenges.

Like the mountain climber who dreams of Everest, the actress who dreams of Hollywood, or the guitar picker who dreams of Nashville, Bob was obsessed with the thought of going to Madison Avenue to call on the big ad agencies. He had heard it was *a different ball game.* Just once, he thought, he'd like to see for himself what it was like in the big leagues.

Alice, Bob's soul-mate, sweetheart, and wife, was the only one who had heard Bob verbalize his secret dream. She encouraged him to go for it.

"Ah Alice," Bob would say, *"it's a whole different ball game up there...why, I wouldn't even know where to start."*

"Well big boy, they play with the same kind of ball, they just throw it faster and hit it further, that's all," Alice came back, *"Why don't you just go sit in the dugout and watch awhile?"*

One night, at two in the morning, Bob woke up shouting, *"You're right Alice, I just need to go sit in the dugout. That's how you make the team, you have to pay your dues, as an understudy to the starters!"*

Alice really didn't know exactly what Bob was saying, but she recognized the gleam in his eyes. In the past, every time he got that gleam, he worked like a mad man for a year or so, then they bought a bigger house.

So, Bob Baker went to New York City. He had no appointment. He didn't know the names of any buyers. But that didn't matter, he didn't have anything to sell. He just went to sit in the dugout.

In New York, Bob invested a week of his vacation sitting in the lobby of the buyer's office at one of New York's leading advertising agencies. The room was filled with sales people, waiting their turn. They talked among themselves, mostly talking shop, as millions of sales people do in the lobbies of thousands of buyer's offices all around the world every day.

Bob Baker, everyone assumed, was just another sales person who was supposed to be there, waiting to see some buyer. They didn't know he was just there to sit in the dugout and clock the pitching. Each day he engaged in conversations with sales people and clerical staff and added to his bag of knowledge about the agency.

It was on his third trip to New York, at the end of the third week Bob had spent in that lobby, unannounced and uninvited, that a salesman from one of the networks asked him who he was there to see. *"Oh, I don't have an appointment with anyone,"* Bob sheepishly replied, *"but I'd love to get one with Mr. Hyde, I've got an idea for one of his clients."*

The network salesman said, *"I'm here to see Bruce Hyde, I'll tell him he ought to talk with you."*

Bob was horrified. He was not ready, and not sure he

19

ever would be. What had started as a fascination with a secret little dream, had led to a response to a challenge from his wife. Now that response was about to put him up to the plate, whether he was ready to hit the pitching or not.

As the network account executive disappeared into the buyer's office, Bob sank down into a chair and started sweating out what he would say to Mr. Hyde if he met him. He knew Bruce Hyde had a reputation for being a tough buyer, a real bear when it came to deal making. Bob also knew Hyde was the primary buyer for the Soapy's account.

Soapy's was an upscale water sports chain. The company sold expensive water sports accessories to rich kids. The lion's share of the company's ad budget went to produce a quarterly catalog that was more of a magazine than catalog. All of this Bob had learned from his time in the dugout and from research he had been doing back home between trips to New York.

Although Bob was a print ad salesman, with no background in any other medium, he had already concluded there had to be a better way to reach rich kids. Hearing his own son pull into the driveway with the CD player turned up to one hundred and fifty-seven million decibels caused an alarm to go off in his head. Soapy's needed to produce a high energy audio version of the catalog, and distribute it to prospects on compact disc, the primary medium of the younger set!

Shock waves traveled through Bob's body at the speed of light when the receptionist called out, *"If there is a Mr. Baker in the office, Mr. Bruce Hyde would like to speak to you on the courtesy phone."*

"This is Bob Baker," Bob said as he picked up the phone.

"Baker, this is Bruce Hyde. Phil Adcock tells me you have something I might want to hear about, can you come back next week?"

A week later, Bob stepped out of the dugout, on to the playing field of Madison Avenue in New York City. He struck out; but, he got invited back. After several more trips to New York, several more calls on Mr. Hyde, and a lot of leg work back home, a year later, he signed a thirty-six million dollar contract! At the rates he had been getting chasing rabbits, thirty six-million dollars would have bought enough newspaper space to wallpaper the Empire State Building.

This story is true. Except that there are no Soapy's Water Sports Shops, there is no Alice, no audio magazine, and no newspaper back home. The buyer is real in this story, but his name is not Bruce Hyde and he does not buy for an advertising agency in New York. Bob Baker is also real, but goes by his actual name, except in the case of this book. The thirty-six million dollars was very real, and so was the dugout. By doing field level research and responding to the pull of the market, the real person characterized by Bob Baker really did make a thirty-six million dollar sale of a product he developed to meet the customer's specific need. One other thing is real: to move up to the next league, you've got to spend some time in the dugout.

Just for you, we have interviewed Billy Bob Baker extensively and picked his brain. He has listed for us all of the disciplines you will need to win in the *Bear Woods*. As Bob is quick to point out, there are no *three easy steps,* or *six habits,* or *ten hard and fast rules* to insure your move to the top levels of sales. The quick and easy steps are for those who chase rabbits. Big league buyers in the bear woods are much more complicated than their counterparts in the minor leagues.

21

They are typically brighter, better educated, more well rounded, and much more motivated and dedicated. They possess a wider array of buying motivations and each must be dealt with differently.

Just as you can become a guitar player by learning a few simple chords, you can become a good salesperson in the minor leagues with just a few skills and a little bit of knowledge. But, to become a master guitarist or concert pianist you have to know all the chords and master all the skills. To become a heavy hitter in the big league of selling you have to expand your knowledge and ability from one end of the scale to the other; you must master all the disciplines of the top level sales professional.

Just as a golf pro must have all the clubs in the bag on every hole, you must hone each discipline so it will be available when needed. Action is fast in the bear woods. On any given call, you will not know ahead of time which skills you will need. Now's the time to make the commitment to have them all polished and ready for every call.

Often at the upper levels of the sales profession, success depends on the sales professional's ability to *feel* out the situation. The more work you do on the disciplines, the better *feel* you will have.

The fact that you are reading this book indicates that you at least have an interest in expanding your knowledge so that you can climb to a higher level. Like a builder building a tall building, you are building your sales career. The taller the building, the more important the foundation. The transition from a good sales professional to a great sales professional requires a complex foundation made of many bricks. Each brick must be in place and interlinked with all the other bricks to provide the strength needed to support the structure. That's why there are no three easy steps. There are, however, many interlocking skills and abilities you must master to reach your goal. The pattern will be different for each call and/or buyer.

This book is not a *how to, hands on, step by step,* listing of *tested and proven* selling methods. We assume you already know how to sell. Improvement now is not a matter of assuming the proper posture or saying the magic words. Moving up now means absorbing the attitude and culture of a master track sales professional. It means mastering the *soft stuff,* like patience, personality, and intense attention to detail.

And while this book is neither *The Bible of Sales,* nor a complete and final works, it is a compilation of the best thoughts of several who have crossed the bridges you want to cross and have reached the lofty goals you seek. Once you have arrived, we hope you will collect your thoughts, draw from your notes, and add to the well of knowledge available to those who follow by sharing your successes through the invitation you will find at the end of this book.

As you read on, make notes and prepare to sharpen your blade. Just a little improvement in each of the areas outlined in this book will make a tremendous difference. Every little detail is a big deal when you sell in the bear woods.

Selling in the Bear Woods

*"The tongue of the just is as choice silver;
the mouth of the just bringeth forth wisdom;
the integrity of the upright shall guide them."*

-SOLOMON

THE FIRST DISCIPLINE

Credibility. This is the *cornerstone*. Big league accounts do not do business with liars, cheats and thieves. They don't do business with people who are remotely tempted to lie, cheat, or steal; or just shade the truth, or even occasionally forget to tell the whole truth.

[Billy Bob Says- *"Eliminate gray areas, deal in facts, without innuendos and insinuations."*]

How honest can you be? Our friend Ralph Hood illustrates the various levels of honesty with these three questions?

> 1) *Would you steal a piece of pie from a restaurant?*

> 2) *If the waiter forgot to put it on your ticket, would you point it out to the cashier?*

> 3) *What if you were fifteen minutes down the road when you realized the waiter forgot to charge you for it, would you go back to pay for the pie?*

With these questions in mind, do you feel there is room for you to hone your level of honesty? Credibility is the benefit you earn by being honest; painfully honest. Credibility is crucial, because people buy from only those they trust. The bigger the order, the more important the level of trust. When it comes to honesty and credibility, there are no little indiscretions in the bear woods.

The primary objective in building a relationship with a

customer is for that customer to feel comfortable with you. Trust is a must. People are not comfortable doing business with people they do not trust.

[Billy Bob Says- *"Opportunities present themselves to salespeople, that buyers feel comfortable with."*]

Remember, the bear woods are home to sophisticated, intelligent buyers who get around, and they talk. If you are less than honest, everyone will know. Unless you travel with the circus and play a different town every week, many of today's sales will come from the people you sold to yesterday. You can irritate a bear only once. You do not get a second chance.

The keys to credibility are judgement and consistency. Judgement means knowing the right thing to do and doing the right thing. Consistency means always knowing and always doing the right thing. Like a small scratch on the hood of a new BMW, one little slip-up can take the luster off your reputation and cost you a lot of money.

Your ability to use good judgement in the heat of negotiations will result in a higher percentage of successful sales and more orders.

Those who take short cuts in the area of honesty may

soar with short term success. However, when the market discovers the truth, like a rocket out of fuel, they drop back to earth almost as quickly as they ascended.

Why the world believes dishonesty, or at least a capacity for passing out mis-information, is an asset to a sales rep, is a mystery to us. Nobody buys anything from someone they cannot trust, with the lone exception of those who tote guns and traffic in contraband. Credibility is absolutely the *first* discipline of sales. Sales people at the highest levels of the profession earn and protect impeccable reputations for credibility. They always pay for the pie!

While you must have a viable product, and you must be able to deliver it and service it at a competitive price, you cannot get to first base without trust. Buyer's who do not trust you will not consider the things you have to sell.

You have heard it said, *It's not what you know, but who you know.* In the bear woods it's not that simple. *It's who knows you, and how they know you.* Before you can earn their business, you have to earn their trust. Your reputation in the bear woods is what the buyers think of you, and what they learn they can expect from you; not who you are, not what you have accomplished, not what you believe, but, what the buyers think of you. Your reputation will have to be earned day by day, and protected day by day. Competitors who would discredit you will be on the constant look-out for cracks in the armor. Any they find will be quickly shared with buyers, other salespeople, and associates.

There is a very bright upside. Buyers spread good news too. Once you have earned credibility with a client, he or she will be willing to vouch for you, and often even suggest to others that they do business with you.

Often a buyer will call on a trusted vendor to ask

advice or to find a source for a particular item or need. This is the big bonus that comes to those who earn reputations for trustworthiness and dependability. It's how many sales people increase sales. Credibility affords opportunity, and creativity brings it to fruition. (We'll talk about creativity later.)

Because of your credibility, you will have opportunities to help buyers source products they need, even when you don't have the product, or access to it. By helping the buyer, you become a *valuable resource for information*.

Selling in the Bear Woods is not a short term proposition. There will be a long term payoff for your efforts to earn the trust and respect of others. Over the course of a career, yours and theirs, people move around. They may move, you may move; more than once. Trusted relationships transcend employers. When they move, you pick up new customers. Credibility is a long term commitment, with long term advantages for those who earn it.

Do you always pay for the pie? Can you always be honest, painfully honest, even when honesty is very expensive? Again, we turn to our friend Ralph Hood for illustration:

Sound Business Ethics

I overheard a group of young folks discussing business the other day and it was sort of sad. It seems those young people sincerely believe that you have to be crooked to succeed in business and; therefore, all successful business people are crooked.

I thought about two of the most successful business people I have ever known, Bob and Dave. This is a true story and those are their real names--Bob and Dave.

Bob and Dave sort of grew up in the aviation business together. They were in different parts of the country and different ends of the business, but they were both industry leaders and each admired the other.

Bob owned a commercial aviation operation in Alabama and Dave had an aviation insurance company in St. Louis. Dave's company insured Bob's company.

As Bob's business grew, Dave tried to sell him a certain special coverage that Bob didn't think he needed. Each year Bob turned him down.

One year, Bob's company had a freak type of accident involving many thousands of dollars. He called Dave and asked, "Am I covered for that?"

"No," Dave said, "that comes under the special coverage I tried to sell you, but you wouldn't buy it."

"I was afraid of that," Bob said, "I'll just have to come up with the money myself."

After the call, Dave, just to be sure, pulled Bob's policy from the files. He didn't have to do that, but he did.

To his absolute amazement, Dave found that, even though Bob had definitely turned it down, the special coverage was on the policy. It was a mistake, but it was on there.

Now remember, Bob had already agreed that he hadn't bought that coverage. Dave didn't have to say a word. He could just put the file back in the drawer and Bob would never know the difference.

Dave called Bob immediately. "Bob," he said, "you'll never believe this. I guess I made a mistake on the original paperwork and you do have the special coverage, even though you didn't want it. It's on the policy, you have been paying the premium for it, and we'll pay for your accident!"

There was a long pause. Then Bob answered, "No, Dave, that's not the deal we made. You send me a refund on the extra premium I've paid and we'll be even!" And, that's how it was handled.

Contributed by Ralph Hood
[Ralph Hood is a professional speaker and seminar leader from Huntsville, AL, and is the author of The Truth & Other Lies]

To business people like Bob and Dave, principle is far more important than profit. To them, the real bottom line is what is said about you after your assets have been divided among your kids and you are gone.

Dave's honesty could have cost him the thousands of dollars it would have taken to pay Bob's claim. Bob's stubborn determination to stick to his principles, his firm belief that *a deal is a deal,* did cost him thousands of dollars!

Would you have done it that way? A lot of people would not; but all who know Bob know that he would. His way is tougher than just paying for the pie. The bear woods are tough; nevertheless, Bob's reputation has earned him a spot as a player in the bear woods.

You've heard the trite sayings:

"You can't make a good deal with a bad guy,"
and
"You have to talk the talk and walk the walk."

These are trite but true. Trite, because they've been

31

around so long. They've been around so long because they are so true.

There's another old saying that applies here. *"Anything short of the whole truth, is not the truth."* This covers all of those times when you are tempted to tell the technical truth and console your conscience with the thought that it's OK to leave out or overlook the things that weren't asked about specifically. If you know it, and you know it's important to your customer, you better tell it, even if it should cost you a deal. It's always better to maintain trust and confidence, even if it causes you to lose a deal today, than to lose the account tomorrow. Failure to be perfectly honest will eventually catch up with you and you'll be bitten by the bear.

Before the first cave man who bought the first wheel asked, *"What will this thing do for me?,"* he asked himself, *"Can I trust this guy who's trying to sell it to me?"* It's the same question you ask yourself before you reach down in your pocket and get out your money to spend it with someone else.

Buying decisions are based on information, much of which is supplied by sellers. Bad information leads to bad decisions. Big time buyers know this very well. Experience got them to the big leagues. They've been burned before. They become extremely cautious critters.

In the bear woods, your credibility will be questioned sooner, and more often, than ever before. Your honesty will be monitored like never before. Your reputation will be more important than ever before. Always pay for the pie, and always leave a tip. It's not a little thing anymore.

Billy Bob Baker's Credibility Checkpoints

▶ *Perception is reality--how do your prospective clients perceive you? What can you do to improve their perception of you?*

▶ *How do your current clients <u>really</u> feel about you? What can you do to make them feel even more comfortable about doing business with you?*

▶ *What can you do today to improve your credibility level among your customers, your associates, and your friends?*

▶ *List five things you will work on, beginning immediately, to insure that you are seen as one who is trustworthy, in the eyes of your clients, your company, and yourself.*

Bear Traps to Avoid

☞ *Avoid even the appearance of dishonesty!*

☞ *Always tell <u>all</u> of the truth!*

It's not what you know, but who you know,
some people like to say.
But I don't think that's the ticket
that will really get you on your way.
It's who knows you, and how they know you,
that's the important test.
Do they know you as someone special,
even those who know you best/
Do you treat them like a brother,
can you be a trusted friend?
Do they see you as a neighbor,
they can trust through thick and thin?
Are you honest and straightforward,
are you always fair and square?
People don't care if they even know you,
until they know how much you care!

-Bryan Townsend

"I am a part of all that I have met."

-TENNYSON

THE SECOND DISCIPLINE

Empathy. When you look out the window, you must see what your customers see. You must learn to see what they see, feel what they feel, and think what they think. When you reach the level where their problems become your problems and you only see opportunity when you see opportunity for them, then you will be ready for the bear woods.

You must become your customer's partner. Partners look out for one another. That's the benefit of partnering. Your customer may not ever consider himself to be your partner, but you better consider yourself to be his. All selling in the bear woods is partnership selling.

You can take responsibility for your sales success by

taking responsibility for the success of your customers. Understand what the buyer needs and wants, assume ownership and accountability for your success and the buyer's success. Partner by helping the buyer see things that are not there yet, but are just over the horizon.

Once you've earned the customer's trust, you can position yourself to be his/her partner. Understand the buyer's situation and work to make it easy for the buyer to say yes, by placing yourself in their situation before you make your presentation. It will work for anyone who sells anything. It just takes the ability to see the world as the customer sees it so you can recognize their needs and concerns.

As a partner, you can constantly plant seeds of excitement about opportunities you have. When the time is right, you can present them and they will grow.

[Billy Bob Says- *Never let'em see you sweat when things are not looking good...and __never__ __ever__ let'em see you grin when things are looking real good.*]

Once, I met a man who had mastered the process. I was standing on the curb at the airport in Savannah with my bag in my hand, when a cab driver jumped out of his cab. With a big grin he said, *"My name is Charlie Thomas and I want to be the first one to welcome you to Savannah! Where do you need to go?"*

"Downtown," I said.

As he took my bag and stuck it in the back of the cab and opened the door for me, Charlie said, *"It's about a fifteen minute drive downtown, but there are some interesting sights along the way."*

Charlie was already seeing the world from my point of reference. He knew I must have been thinking, *how long is this going to take, is the ride going to be boring?* From the airport to the hotel, he pointed out sights like a tour guide.

When we pulled up to the door of the Hilton, Charlie turned and asked, *"When will you be going back to the airport?"* Sure, he was lining up a future fare, but he was doing it by solving a problem for me, his new partner.

"Tomorrow morning," I said.

"What time tomorrow morning?" he asked.

"Seven-thirty tomorrow morning," I answered.

"Well, don't you worry about calling a cab," Charlie said, *"because tomorrow morning at seven-thirty, this cab is going to be right here, I'm gonna be waiting on you!"*

That is customer service! Making it easy for your customers to do business with you. You do that by seeing the world from your customer's point of reference, staying a jump ahead, anticipating their wants and needs, taking on the role of a partner who provides support, cover and backup.

The next morning at seven-fifteen I stepped out of the elevator, into the lobby of the DeSoto Hilton in downtown Savannah. Standing over by the desk, waiting on me, was Charlie Thomas. I looked at my watch and said, *"Charlie, you are a little early this morning."*

"Oh, don't you worry about me," he said. *"You get some breakfast if you want to, I just wanted to be early in case you needed to go early!"*

That is the essence of partnership selling--anticipating

customer wants and needs, and supplying readily available options to fill those wants and needs. Those who do it best are the ones who thrive in the bear woods.

A million cabbies go to bed each night wondering if they will find an early fare in the morning--not Charlie Thomas. Because of his empathy and his willingness to partner with his customers, it was rare for Charlie, (during his long tenure as a cab driver in Savannah), to go to bed without several trips already lined up for the next day. You see, Charlie was a master at asking *the next question.*

There is always one more question that can be asked to ascertain the needs of customers. Bob Baker always keeps one tucked back, to use when he can't think of any other pertinent question for the moment. It's Billy Bob's never fail, always powerful, empathetic approach, partnership selling technique. He has given permission for us to share it with you:

"Is there something I need to be working on for you?"

Bob says he cannot count the times this question has led to additional sales. You see, once you have earned the trust and respect of the prospect, earned the business and then earned a spot on the team as your customer's partner, you will find they will want to turn to you rather than risk dealing with those they do not know. Bob calls this *the big bonus in the bear woods.*

While it's tough to hit the pitching in the big leagues, once you learn to do it, everybody will want to see you come up to bat. That's why it's worth the effort and worth the risk for you to move up to the next level in your profession. The road is steep and the climb is hard, but once you get there, the view is wonderful!

Empathy is the trait that, more than any other, will help you master partnership selling. It is essential in developing the strong foundation, which you need to reach the next level in your profession.

In order to work toward mastery of this area, answer this question as it relates to each of your prospects:

What are the greatest concerns this customer has right now, and what can I do to help?

Credibility is the first discipline. You can't become a great sales professional without it. Empathy is the second. Credibility earns trust, empathy earns respect. Only those who are trusted and respected survive in the bear woods. These alone will not insure success; but, the lack of either will doom you to failure, sooner or later.

Billy Bob's Suggestions
for
Increasing Empathy

▶ *Always place yourself in the buyer's position.*

▶ *Before you say something to your buyer, be ready to answer the question-- "so what?"*

Bear Traps to Avoid

▶ *Don't get labeled as a phony by displaying false empathy, always be genuine.*

▶ *Don't withhold options, give the buyer all the facts and let him make his own decisions.*

*"Know how to listen, and you will profit
even from those who talk badly."*

-PLUTARCH

THE THIRD DISCIPLINE

Be a good listener. Information is critical. Most of us are not born with good listening skills. Since early childhood we have been crying out to be heard. But, great sales people know, you have to listen to sell. How well do you listen? Do you always pick up people's names, the first time you hear them? Do you always refrain from comment until the other party has said all they want to say at the time? Are you listening to what they are saying, or planning your response?

[Billy Bob Says- *"The quickest and easiest way to sell something is to ask a lot of questions and LISTEN."*]

The best way to incrementally increase an already good account is to listen and react. Many times a buyer will mention a need and you have exactly the right item and know it is right for the buyer. At other times, the buyer will mention something and you will have to develop an item or solution to meet the need. In all cases, when the buyer mentions a need, immediately think, "Yes!", then do whatever it takes to solve the buyer's problem and meet his or her need.

Without your full understanding of what prospects want or need, you cannot help them achieve their goals. Aggressive listening and thorough questioning will help identify key things you need to give customers what they want.

Again, ours is not so much a *how to* approach as it is a *how come* approach. The *how come* here is very simple. To be a better sales person, you have to be an even better listener. You can get there; but, it will require time on task. Start now monitoring your performance, charting a course for improvement, and measuring your progress. Go back to the book store and purchase some good books on improving your listening and memory skills. Invest time on task. Prospects perceive you to be more empathetic when they realize you are hearing and understanding what they say.

It's important to hear not only what is said; but also, what is not said. Often the things a prospect does not say drop clues for the artful listener. Gleaning information in the sales arena is vitally important. Ascertaining wants, needs, goals, and objectives leads to the ability to make more targeted presentations, more specific offers, and thus increases your odds for successfully fulfilling the customer's needs.

The Value of Silence

Too often sales people will ask good questions; but, then proceed to step on top of the buyer's opportunity to fully respond with information. Shut up, listen, and learn!

Effective listening should always interlock with the first two disciplines of credibility and empathy. It's only when your customers trust you, and feel you understand them, that they will truly begin to open up and share information with you. When they do, this leads to an exchange of information which will put you in a position to become a valuable source of solutions for them.

Then, as a partner, you can become a major provider of information needed by the customer. It may be information about products, about the competition, or about the marketplace. Listening to customers lets you learn what they need, and listening to others helps you meet those needs.

From the story of Billy Bob, we learned his move to the big leagues started with a few trips to the lobby of the buyer's office, just to listen to the marketplace. It ended with a $36,000,000.00 sale!

Lew was another good listener. In his bait shop, he learned that the local fishermen needed stronger fishing poles. Often they'd complain that the pole broke and the big one got away.

In his shop, Lew learned he could heat-temper a cane pole with a blow torch to make it stronger. He sold over a million of them at a dollar each! While the major players in the fishing tackle industry were searching for ways to make tackle cheaper, Lew heard the marketplace say it wanted better tackle. So he invested his cane pole earning into product development and introduced the world's first graphite fishing rod. A billion dollar industry was born, because a salesman in a bait shop in Lower Alabama was listening to his customers.

[Billy Bob Says- *"Listening is important in securing vital information for you to sell the right product, position your presentation in the most positive light, and pull the trigger on closing the deal."*]

Accumulating information-good, accurate, pertinent

information-is the key to selling *master-track* buyers. Asking questions, observing reactions, and aggressively listening are three essential steps to ascertaining the information needed to sell in the bear woods.

Suggestions for Improving Your Listening Skills

▶ *Find good books & tapes on this subject, read them, listen to them, and take them to heart.*

▶ *Listening is vitally important, but dies on the vine if you don't respond and/or react to what the buyer says--action is what the buyer wants.*

▶ *Practice makes perfect. Practice catching names and other important data the first time you hear it said.*

Bear Traps to Avoid

▶ *Do not assume you know; ask the customer more questions to verify your understanding.*

▶ *Do not fail to verify information you obtain from from shop talk with those in your industry, or through any source you are not completely sure about.*

▶ *Never give a customer or prospect anything less than your undivided attention when they are talking to you.*

"They laugh that win."

-SHAKESPEARE

THE FOURTH DISCIPLINE

Command of a likable personality. Now, it's time for a personality check. You do not have to be the life of the party. In fact, the outgoing personality that works well in the minor leagues can be a liability in the big leagues. Substance overrides style in the bear woods. However, you must be likable, and non-threatening.

Start by assessing your personality. What are the strengths and weaknesses of your personality? What can you do to improve any weak personality traits, and what can you do to best utilize your strengths?

Hone your people skills. You must come across as one who has good self-esteem and a good self-image but is not overconfident.

[Billy Bob Says- *Overconfidence is perceived as being cocky, and that is not a personality trait* *people* *like.*]

Overbearing sales people can do well pushing rabbits. You cannot push bears. It takes finesse to put orders in the barrel at the upper levels. Selling in the bear woods is like riding a wild stallion. You hold on for a while and you spur for a while. The likable personality allows you to hang on while the stallion is bucking.

You must acquire the personality of a diplomat. Diplomats have tough skin. They do not flinch in the face of setbacks and they know how to keep their cool when they come under fire.

Early in our careers, there was a politician in our area who was constantly in the center of controversy. He was a marked man in the eyes of the news media; but, he was beloved by the voters and always bounced back at election time, because he had tough skin and held his cool under fire. You could cuss him, and kick him, and spit in his face; but he'd always respond with a boyish grin and a compliment for you. It's hard not to like a guy like that, and that's your goal, to polish your personality and toughen your skin to the point

48

it's even hard for your competitors not to like you.

As you work to master this area, learn to grin at adversity. Jimmy Joe Woodard, another great sales professional, always grinned when he was attacked by temper, frustration, fear or any other threatening emotion. Often his grin would relax the other party, and emotions on both sides would give way to reason, and negotiation could resume.

While you do not have to be the life of the party, a million laughs, a great golfer or a whiz at ping pong, you must be pleasant. You must have a pleasing personality whether it is natural or acquired. The best way to improve your personality is to learn to be gracious.

Master
The High Art of Graciousness

In your hometown, if you grew up in any except the largest cities, there was an old doctor you remember from your past who was respected, almost revered by the community. Every town had one, everybody's favorite old doctor.

A young doctor could come in and spend five minutes with you, scoot out the door, and you'd feel like your problem was not the least concern of the doctor's. On the other hand, the old doc everybody loved could come in, spend the same five minutes, and make you feel like he had all the time in the world, just for you.

For one thing, the old doctor knew how to be attentive. He listened to you, not only with his ears; but, with his eyes.

49

He didn't check the charts or check his watch while you were talking to him and he made you feel special. For these reasons, he earned the respect of the community and everybody said he had a *good bedside manner.*

The respected old doctor was practicing the art of graciousness. It's practiced by the world's greatest doctors, doormen, and diplomats. It will be practiced by you when you achieve success in the bear woods.

Joel Alderman, is a car dealer and a master at the art of graciousness. When he calls on the telephone, he always starts by saying, *"I sure hope I'm not interrupting something important."* With this phrase, he's showing his empathy, letting you know he respects you and is aware that his phone call could be intruding on your time. His graciousness earns your respect and makes you want to have him around to rely on for suggestions and advice anytime you are in the market for a new vehicle.

Joel never takes the spotlight. In his presence, he always makes you feel like you are the life of the party. He not only listens to the things you say, but becomes genuinely interested in you and the things that are important to you. His pleasant personality interlocks well with his excellent listening skills and his genuine empathy.

Use Your Sense of Humor

Humor is a great tool for *master-track* sales people. As part of your personality, you should develop your ability to be funny, witty, humorous and amusing. All of these will be effective from time to time in gaining attention, diffusing controversy, and making valid points. Just remember, in today's bear woods, only tasteful humor is accepted.

Remember to keep your good personality on display at all times. It's not there just for today's buyers. Today's stock boys, clerks, and secretaries will become tomorrow's buyers, sooner than you think.

Many sales people have done well in the minor leagues using the power of their personality alone. In the majors, you have to have the personality, and you must interlink it with your other skills. Here, a few chords are not enough, you've got to play the whole keyboard.

In the minor leagues they often say, *"People buy from people they like."* There's some truth to that at all levels of selling. However, in the arena where you aspire to play, reality reads more into the quote, so that it comes out like this:

"Master track buyers prefer to buy from master track sales professionals they like, who have mastered all of the disciplines, including control of a pleasing personality."

Our individual personality charateristics define us as a person; and customers too, or defined by their personality characteristics. These characteristics are powerful forces that affect the way we see, and hear, and understand. Consequently they have enormous effects on decisions we make, most especially buying decisions.

Jimmy Woodard and I used to team sell. When either of us ran into a buyer who just didn't seem to *like* one of us, that one would back off and the other would pick up the account. In twenty years of selling together, we never ran into a prospect that had a personality conflict with both of us.

You must learn to analyze the personalities of your individual customers. Knowing and understanding their individuality helps you tailor the right approach when you deal with them in the various stages of the selling relationship.

Every Buyer is Different

Dan was a crusty old buyer with an extremely caustic personality. He marched around like a drill sergeant and barked at everyone around him. His personality was such that he always wanted to feel in control.

The young salesman who had been assigned to call on Dan had tried everything, with no success. He couldn't get to first base. One afternoon, on a reluctant call, the young man opened with what the textbook salesperson would call the worst possible line, *"You don't want to buy anything do you Dan?"*

Dan responded, *"Oh yes I do, where in the heck have you been?"*

It was an accidental find, but the young man learned Dan liked to be contemptuous so much, a negative approach afforded him an opportunities to bully you into letting him buy.

Some buyers seek control while some want you to be in control. Some buyers want peace while others thrive on conflict. Certain buyers are moved by reason & logic while others must be moved with emotion. They're all different. Their individual personalities are the key to the difference. Your control and use of your personality as you interelate with

them as individuals will be a major factor in determining your
level of success in the high and noble craft of selling.

Tips
for Improving
Your Sales Personality

*1) Practice holding your cool under fire. Grin first,
get the facts, then react.*

*2) Concentrate on making the other party feel like
the center of attention.*

*3) In all situations, think about the doctor, the
doorman, and the diplomat and how they
would play it.*

Bear Traps to Avoid

▶ *Do not become predictable.*

▶ *Never try to cover your shortcomings with confidence, as you will be perceived as cocky.*

▶ *Be very cautious with humor, and always maintain good taste.*

▶ *Personality strengths carried to the extreme become a weakness.*

"Knowledge is of two kinds.

We know a subject ourselves,
or we know where we can find
information upon it. "

-SAMUEL JOHNSON

THE FIFTH DISCIPLINE

Knowledge. You must know a little something about what you are selling to chase rabbits. You must know *everything* about what you are selling to sell in the bear woods.

Information about the product itself is good; but, if buyer's only wanted information about products, they could call for a brochure or look it up on the Internet. Knowledge about the buyer's needs, and being able to explain what the product will do to service them is much more important.

Bob Baker earned commissions as a newspaper advertising salesman for years, before he knew anything about advertising. He knew about his newspaper. He knew all the circulation numbers and he could figure column inches. However, Bob had made a thorough study of the wrong things.

While Bob was selling newspaper space, his customers were buying advertising. When he realized this and improved his product knowledge by learning how to use advertising to help his customers reach their goals, he became an even better sales person.

Instead of trying to start at ground zero, Bob went to the masters. The great masters of the past (in all professions) have blessed us by leaving written accounts behind in the form of memoirs, biographies and other published works. Bob read, not only the text books and periodicals of the trade; but also, studied the masters. Doing this made him an authority on the subject when compared to his competitors.

First you want to master product knowledge. What is it you sell? (You can't know too much about it; even though most of your knowledge may never be verbalized to your customers.) Then you must know all you can know about uses and applications of the product and/or service. All of this information will be used by you to meet customer needs and discover new sales opportunities.

Marolyn Wright is a successful master track sales professional from Louisville, Kentucky. She's the founder and owner of a respected speakers bureau that helps meeting planners select speakers for their events. She will not recommend a speaker for her clients unless she has heard the speaker herself. Then she knows what the speaker can do for her clients.

Marolyn has been known to travel great distances, just to preview a speaker before recommending that speaker to a client. On one occasion she flew to Miami to watch a seminar leader at work before recommending him to one of her customers. This is the kind of thing she does on a regular basis to make sure her customers get first class service from her. This gives her first hand product knowledge, the kind you need to make it in the bear woods.

In addition to all the hard facts about your product, you must know how the product relates to your goals and your customer's goal. Never push a product that is not right for you or your customer. Always try to take *winners* to your buyers. Like a wise farmer who spends most of his time on his most fertile ground, know your products well enough to maximize your time and efforts.

[Billy Bob Says- *"Master track sales professionals focus their efforts on items and ideas that present major opportunity."*]

Knowledge is the discipline that enables you to spot major opportunities. Being known as knowledgeable puts you in a position to rise to the top.

Partnership Selling

When the buyer perceives you as a partner, the buyer will come to you as a major source of information. At that point, you will have successfully interlinked product knowledge with the other important disciplines. Earning a reputation as an authority in your industry gets you to this position. By your being a source for information, buyers will know they can come to you and get advice and information they cannot readily get anywhere else. The information may be about products, competition, companies, or even things totally unrelated to what you sell or service. When they perceive you as a partner, they will be much more likely to come to you for help with their problems--for anything they need.

The Four C's of Partnership Selling

Concept-   *Both parties must understand the objective.*

Communicate-   *Both parties must be able to communicate effectively and timely to get the right answers to the right questions and do the right things for both parties.*

Confidence-   *Both sides must have respect for each other and confidence in one another, so that each is comfortable in knowing the other knows what is needed for both to win.*

Cooperate-   *Both must be determined and flexible enough to do what it*

takes to get the job done,
working together to achieve the
mutually beneficial goal.

Too many negotiations begin and end with the buyer and seller in an adversarial relationship. The buyer is sure the seller has a better deal and negotiates hard to get it. The seller is afraid to quote the best deal first because many buyers refuse to take the first offer. In partnership selling, you develop a relationship where you and the buyer work together to develop the product or program, secure the right selling point, and work backwards toward the selling price.

The burden of building this relationship rests upon the seller. The key you will use to get you there will be your reputation for honesty, reliability, production, and knowledge.

Selling is not knowing your products or services, positioning them in the best light, presenting them to your prospects, and expecting an order. Selling is working backwards from the prospect's position regarding his/her needs, and customizing your products, programs, and services to best fit those needs.

Now, who is the foremost authority in your industry? You should be among the top few. Research, study, and time on task will get you there. The view from the top is well worth the effort.

Customer Knowledge

Even more important than product knowledge is knowledge about your potential customers. What is their value to you? Can they put you in the big leagues if you put together the right items for them? Target customers who can buy in volume and get you where you need to be. You can't sell in the bear woods if you keep chasing rabbits. Master track sales pros have the knowledge to manage return on investment. They understand it is often unwise to spend time and money without the potential of profitable returns.

Too often, salespeople feel comfortable where they are, and are not willing to step out of their comfort zones. This factor alone keeps many potential master track sales pros out of the bear woods. They're like the fisherman who stays in the pond catching the little fish because he's too timid to venture out into the ocean.

Superior knowledge and information is a major key to success in the bear woods. How do buyers buy? Who is the real decision maker? What motivates them to purchase something? What are they looking for? When is the best time to make your move? What problems are their competitors causing them? How can you help?

Knowing the answers to the questions above will prepare you to venture out into the ocean--hunt in the Bear Woods. Knowlede is power in sales.

Billy Bob's
Knowledge Checkup

▶ *Analyze & know your strengths & weaknesses.*

▶ *Find ways to maximize your strengths & work around weaknesses.*

▶ *Stay focused on your area of expertise.*

▶ *Learn as much as you can about your customers & prospects.*

▶ *Do whatever it takes to become recognized by your customers as an authority in your industry.*

Bear Traps to Avoid

▶ *Be cautious not to appear as a know-it-all.*

▶ *Never get caught acting like you know, when in reality you do not.*

▶ *Be careful to relate your knowledge to customers in terms they understand.*

▶ *Never assume customers understand your motives. Be sure to show your customers that you care about them because, customers do not care how much you know until they know how much you care.*

"Drowsiness shall clothe a man with rags."

-PROVERBS

THE SIXTH DISCIPLINE

Drive. Good things rarely ever happen by accident, most often they happen on purpose. Somebody has to get up off of it and do something to make good things happen. Knowledge may be power, but power only makes noise until you harness it with a transmission and drive train.

Like the rose bud blooming in the desert, the greatest products and grandest ideas are wasted until someone introduces them to the marketplace. The sharpest axe cuts nothing until it is lifted above the log. Master track sales professionals are the ones who identify opportunities and take action to introduce great products and grand ideas.

It is so important to push to get things done. Great danger lies in assuming you have plenty of time to get an item or an idea accomplished. The buyer may be on a faster timetable than you, your competition may be a step ahead. Either situation will cost you money; in the short run--today's sale. In the long term scope of things, your delay could cost you future business and opportunities that might have manifested themselves because of that sale.

Jimmy Joe Woodard says, *"The road to success is wide open at four o'clock in the morning."* Many of the great sales people we know rise early to read, write, learn, and prepare themselves for the day. It has been said that he who rises an hour early each day, and spends that extra hour reading about his industry, a year later becomes known as an authority on the subject.

Likewise, the individual who acts and does find an hour a day, either in the morning or evening, to study and hone his or her craft, eventually becomes a leader in their field. While an hour a day seems like a small investment, the rewards can be enormous.

Motivational speaker Les Brown says, *"You can't become what you want to be if you continue to be what you have been."* Changing yourself, improving your skills, and increasing you level of knowledge requires *time on task*. Remember, at the master track level, *it's the little things that make the big difference.* Finding time to invest in themselves is one of the little things successful people do to grow--to stand out above the rest.

There is no reason why you should not be one of the most widely read persons in your industry. Read all the good books and all the trade peridocials that relate to what you do and what you provide for your customers. Establish relationships with the leaders in the industry, learn from them and become an authority.

Shifting Into Overdrive

When your car shifts into overdrive, it does not apply more power. The transmission changes to use the power that's available more effectively. This is similar to the process master track sales professionals use to optimize their effectiveness in the bear woods. They do work harder, but they also work *smarter.*

An accomplished sales manager at the highest level shared the following with us:

"I see it everyday, salespeople or regional sales managers working hard, busy as bees, putting in long hours, but only achieving minimal results. Why? Because they confuse their high level of activity with a high level of accomplishment. At the entry level of selling, and even into the mid levels of the profession, big doses of activity can be enough to help you become successful; but, once you reach the master level of selling, activity alone will not allow you to achieve master results. Only clear cut goals and directions help eliminate unnecessary activity. If an activity does not move you closer to the desired result, don't do it. Time is too precious at this level. Without strategic planning and a clear map, confusing activity with achievement is inevitable. Action, (moving toward the strategic goal), in conjunction with a good attitude is eighty-five per cent of success in selling. The remaining fifteen percent is product or technical

knowledge. Sales people get into trouble and waste time when this gets reversed.

Master track sales professionals realize that the road is steep. If it was all downhill, everybody would be well on their way to success. It can be tough climbing to the top; but, for the pros willing to pay the price, the rewards are great.

In the minor leagues, *a can-do* attitude is lauded as a great virtue. However, at the mastery level, it's not enough.

[Billy Bob Says- ***"Can-do has to become do, do; you must take action and do all the things you know to do."*]**

The master of martial arts does not earn the black belt for knowing all the moves. The belt is won by those who execute all the moves. A map will reveal the route up the mountain, but you have to climb it yourself to enjoy the view from the top.

A few years back, our friend Ralph Hood sold an airplane to a race car driver, former NASCAR Grand National Champion Bobby Allison. You can imagine, a race car driver would not want a small, single engine airplane. Bobby wanted a fast, twin engine, Piper Aerostar.

And, Bobby wanted some features not normally available on the Aerostar. For one thing, he wanted a

66

speedometer that registers *miles per hour*. Speedometers on airplanes register in knots. Since, Bobby was used to driving a race car, he wanted to know how fast the airplane was going in his terms.

Consequently, the plane had to be special ordered. Anything that has to be ordered special requires extra time. Bobby is a race car driver. Patience is not his long suit. He's always in a hurry.

Every few days he'd call Ralph and ask if the airplane had arrived. Finally, one day it came in. Ralph called Bobby at his shop in Hueytown and said, *"Bobby, your airplane came in this morning. I can deliver it this afternoon."*

Bobby said, *"Ralph, don't bring my airplane this afternoon, I'll be in the sauna this afternoon. Bring the airplane tomorrow morning."*

Ralph could not imagine what this hard charging, macho race car driver would be doing laid back in the sauna, so he asked, *"Bobby, what in the world are you going to be doing in the sauna?"*

Bobby replied, *"Two weeks from now, we're going to be in Daytona, racing in the Firecracker 400. When we get down to Daytona Beach, Florida, the first week in July, it's going to be hot. The temperature is going to be high, the humidity is going to be high, and when I'm in that car, out on that track, and the engine of that race car is producing the horsepower to propel the car around the track at racing speeds, that engine is going to be creating a lot of heat, and all of that heat is going to be coming right back in my face. Between now and then, I'm going to sit in that sauna everyday, as long as I can with it as hot as I can stand it. When those other drivers, from South Carolina, North Carolina, Virginia, and all across this country get down to*

67

Daytona Beach, they're going to be asking themselves if they can take the heat. I'm going to know I can take the heat!"

Master track sales professionals realize it is not enough to simply want to succeed, you *must* prepare to be successful. They have the drive that forces them to plan and prepare, study and learn, step out of their comfort zone, expand the envelope, and test the edge. The result of the drive that forces them to continue to move forward in their careers, gives them the confidence required to take the risks necessary to ascend from level to level until the peak of the profession is obtained.

[Billy Bob Says- *"Risk Not, Gain Not--If you ain't got the drive it takes to be a thoroughbred, you'd better stay out of the Derby."*]

It takes endless drive and unflinching persistence to make it on the fast track. For this reason, many mediocre sales people, and even good sales people, never make it to the top, because they cannot, or will not, exercise the personal drive it takes to master all the disciplines of the art.

You have to have the drive described as *fire in the belly,* and you have to be as persistent as a yellow jacket.

Persistence

*Persistence is the power that allows a little bee
to make a big ole jackass turn around and flee.
It keeps the humming bird from falling to the ground,
and allows a little tugboat to turn a ship around.*

-Bryan Townsend

A veteran sales professional shared the following story about the power of persistence:

John was a haberdasher. While he was on my account list, one of his friends was my competitor. Consequently, I could never get to first base. With determination, I called on him weekly for years. And, although I did not give up, after a number of years those weekly calls became monthly calls, then seasonal calls. After eighteen years, he bought. John became a valued account. It took a long time to get him, but as I look back, I count this as one of my greatest triumphs.

[Billy Bob Says- *"Make your most difficult buyer your personal challenge!"*]

Realize of course, everyday is not your best day. Some days it's wise to take a hike, go fishing, or play golf. As Jimmy Joe Woodard used to say on days like this, *"I ain't got no business doing business today!"* On days when you are sick, feeling down, or simply just not at your best for any number of reasons, don't tackle your most important tasks.

Another master track sales champion shared the following:

Some days you are on top of the world, and the very next day something has changed and the world is on top of you. This is especially so in selling. In terms of emotional power, it can be a very demanding profession. There are always so many factors, beyond your control, that can affect the process: late trucks, lost orders, wrong pricing, incorrect billing, rude customer service people, aggressive competition, personal problems encountered by buyers, and on, and on and on. Many things affect the highs and lows of selling. You have to understand this and stay focused. Long term success is gained by relishing the highs, celebrating the victories, and working quickly through the lows. At times it may become necessary to give up on a particular prospect or some project, but your never surrender you career goals. Set your sights for the mountain top, even when you are down in the valley. By staying focused on your main objectives, you can keep the lows in perspective and drive on toward the finish line.

Master track sales people do not give up when it comes to long term objectives--ever. They realize with deep conviction that *"No"* at worse means *"Not Today,"* and in the face of despair, depression and defeat, they rise back up and utter the words made famous by Scarlet O'Hara in <u>Gone With the Wind</u>, *"Tomorrow will be another day."*

Five Things You Can Do
to
Turn Up Your Drive

1) Define ambitious goals you feel you must achieve, and set deadlines.

2) Determine what preparation you must make to achieve these goals.

3) Set aside one hour daily to prepare.

4) At the end of each day, ask yourself, "What did I accomplish today?" If a good answer is not there, become more determined to make something happen tomorrow.

5) Start now and do not quit!

Bear Traps to Avoid

▶ *Avoid burn out by setting aside time to relax and* unwind.

▶ *Do not neglect your family and friends. Success would be empty without them.*

▶ *Keep your drive under control. Remember the Theory of the A Sharp (you can fine tune an A Sharp until it becomes a B Flat) so as not to run over colleagues and customers.*

THE SEVENTH DISCIPLINE

Confidence. You'd be unwise to venture into the bear woods if you weren't confident. Bears are unforgiving. One mistake and you'd be lunch.

The master track sales professional gains confidence from mastery of the many sales disciplines. Time on task, and developing your assets in all of the other areas, tends to build your strength in this area. This is another case of the interlocking principle. Bricks stacked upon bricks have no strength without the mortar that holds them together as they support one another.

Likewise, we've found, confidence in one area leads to confidence that you can master other areas. As the beginning guitar player learns to play one chord, he learns through experience that he has the ability to learn more chords.

In any field, a master exudes confidence. In professional selling, genuine confidence encourages colleagues, reassures customers, and strikes fear in the hearts of unprepared competitors.

[Billy Bob Says- *"Confidence comes from knowing your product, knowing your customer, and knowing you have done your homework--when you know you can hit the pitching, you are anxious to get up to bat."*]

Personal confidence comes from the time and effort you spend to develop your personal potential. Confidence in your products comes from product knowledge and the wisdom to eliminate or change products that are not right for your customers. In the end, confidence is the result of planning, preparation, and experience.

Role playing is one of the best techniques for developing confidence for a presentation. Playing *devil's advocate* highlights areas of concern and prepares you to answer the hard questions and handle the tough situations.

Just before an important presentation to a customer,

many master track professionals take a few moments of silence, alone, to visualize success. This little extra step before the call works wonders to inject confidence into the emotions; especially, when confidence has already been injected into the logic circuits of the brain through adequate preparation.

As you spend time on task, working to develop your skills in each of the areas outlined in this book, you will find yourself becoming more and more confident. Like a snow ball rolling downhill, the newly found confidence will lead to greater efforts on your part and even more newfound confidence. Logarithmically, a little difference becomes a big difference.

Confidence in yourself, your products, and ideas will translate into enthusiasm. As Will Rogers said, *"People are persuaded more by you because of the depth of your conviction than by the height of your logic; more because of your enthusiasm than anything you say."*

A master track buyer related the following to us:

After saying no to a particular item presented by a good salesman, the salesman thanked me for my time, and then left. I was actually disappointed that he did not push harder for the sale. I really wanted to buy the item; but, I didn't. If the salesman really believed it was the right item, he would have fought harder for the sale.

If you do not have confidence in the things you sell, quit today! Sell something else. You can't win a race riding a slow horse and you can't make it as a sales champion trying to push a losing product. Sell something you really believe in, and never give up. When you have total confidence in the products you are selling, you will find it much easier to convey your enthusiasm to your prospects and convince them of the product's value.

Confidence comes from being excited about what you do. A few years ago, the Auburn Tigers played Michigan in the Sugar Bowl. Michigan led the whole game, right down to the last few seconds.

In the final minutes of the game, Auburn put together a drive that stalled within the shadows of the goal line and timeout was called with just a few seconds left in the game. Trailing by two points, Auburn sent in place kicker Al DelGreco. The kick was good and Auburn pulled out a come-from-behind victory.

Just after the game, on the sidelines, a television reporter interviewed DelGreco. Placing the microphone in this young man's face, the reporter said, *"What were you thinking? You must have been nervous when they called your number and sent you into the game?"*

"Nervous?," DelGreco exclaimed, *"No! I wasn't nervous! All of my life I have dreamed of an opportunity to kick a last second field goal and win an important game. I wasn't nervous, I was excited!"*

Al was confident because he was prepared, and there is no shortcut for preparation. Confidence depends upon it, rests on it, and does not happen without it. Do your homework, be confident. Get excited about the opportunity that follows. Succeed and be happy.

How You Can Increase
Your Confidence Level

Plan-   Identify the steps it will take to reach a certain goal.

Prepare-   Take action to obtain all that is necessary to cover the steps identified in your plan.

Practice-   Go through the process both mentally and physically many times so when
your   time comes to perform, you'll be familiar with the process.

These are the things teams do when they practice, athletes do when they train, and performers do when they rehearse. When you know you've got a winning game plan, and you know you have prepared to execute that game plan, you do not have pre-game jitters. You are excited about the opportunity and you can't wait for the game to begin.

Mastery of this discipline comes, not when you become totally confident in yourself and your products, but when you have stacked all the bricks together and start reaping the rewards that come when your *customers* have total confidence in you. When this occurs, they will start bringing opportunities to you, much like a quarterback who always turns to his clutch receiver when he sees the blitz coming.

Bear Traps to Avoid

▶ *Do not listen to those who say you can't do it.*

▶ *Avoid generalities that cause loss of confidence; focus on goals that breed confidence.*

▶ *Be cautious not to undermine confidence by setting unreasonable qoals and quotas.*

"Next to knowing when to seize an opportunity, the most important thing in life is to know when to forego an advantage."

-DISRAELI

THE EIGHTH DISCIPLINE

Adaptability. Life is an adventure. Things change. The unforseen pops up. When this happens, master track professionals are steady in the water. They do not let panic upset their program. They are able to adapt because they have a clear cut focus on where they are going and what they want to accomplish. The method or road to get there may not always be clear and they must be able to swerve when needed, but they stay focused on the big picture. Real pros know there is always more than one way to get from point A to point B, the route is never as important as the destination, so when the bridge is out they develop an effective *Plan B*.

Although unexpected change may cause stress, it also makes successful selling professionals stretch and grow. It makes them reach out and find more solutions and a sensible plan for overcoming the unexpected obstacles and to take full advantage of unexpected opportunities. Ultimately, the result is sales people made better by the experience, and a company made stronger because of the re-focused common bond that occurs when people achieve victory in spite of great obstacles, together.

Back in the mid '70's, stock car racing crews had learned how to build race cars that were too fast to run safely even on the super speedways of the NASCAR circuit. Switching to *Plan B*, NASCAR officials came up with a new rule which restricted the flow of fuel into the engine, thus holding the cars to safer speeds.

While being interviewed about the rule change, Mr. Bill France, Sr., founder and president of NASCAR at that time, was asked how it would affect racing? He commented, *"It will slow them down for a while"*; but, went on to say, *"If we make'em put sewing machine engines in the cars, sooner or later they'd get'em back up over 200 mph!"*

Having grown up in the sport, Mr. France knew the determined *adaptability* of racing crews. The crews swerved, but never lost focus of their goal to outrun the other guy. They all went to work on various *Plan B's* and just a few years later, NASCAR had to change the rule again, placing even further restrictions on the flow of fuel, because speeds were right back up to where they had been before the initial restriction.

Sam Walton's Three Beliefs

According to David Glass, Chairman and CEO of Wal-Mart Corporation, Sam Walton built his business to unprecedented success on three core beliefs. The first two are based on the power of adaptability.

> **1) Everyday, Sam tried to improve something.**
>
> **2) Sam was willing to take risks and learn from failure.**
>
> **3) Sam believed ordinary people are capable of extraordinary performance.**

Legendary football coach Bear Bryant used to say you have to have a plan for everything. That's part of adaptability, being prepared for the unexpected--always having a Plan B, and having a plan for formulating a new plan in the face of adversity. If you are prepared for adversity, when it pops up, panic does not set in. As the old saying goes, *plan for the best, prepare for the worst, and pray that it falls somewhere in between.*

[Billy Bob Says- *"It's critical for you to be flexible and quick on your feet; to be able to swivel-hip through dangerous territory, and you must have a plan for everything."*]

Several years ago, when hurricane Andrew struck south Florida, Allen Stevens and his executive staff at Florida Seed Company were counting their blessings. Florida Seed, at the time, was based in Ocala, Florida, a safe distance north of the devastation left by Andrew.

Then, one among the group raised the question, *"What if the hurricane had struck here?"* All agreed the company would have been devastated with no plan for such a catastrophe. As tragic story after tragic story continued to pour out of south Florida about families and businesses that literally lost everything, Allen and his staff decided that any prudent business organization, especially in an area prone to such natural disasters, should have a contingency plan.

A committee was organized, and a potential scenario for any conceivable disaster was developed. A master plan including a periodically updated list of vacant office buildings and warehouses in the area was produced. Copies were stored both at the office, and in the homes of the various executives, as well as in a safe deposit box.

A year later, Allen was out of town attending a

conference. It was Saturday night when he received an emergency phone call. Florida Seed Company was on fire! The fire was all consuming and there was nothing left of the company's office and warehouse complex except ashes.

Later that night, when Allen arrived back in Ocala, fire fighters were still on the scene spraying water on flaming timbers. Allen's team was already at work preparing to get back into business.

During the night, an executive command center was set up in Allen's den at his home in Ocala. By morning, office space had been secured and the company's entire staff had been summoned to help set up shop in both the temporary office space and temporary warehouse found from the list in the contingency plan.

By noon Sunday, computers were up and running with the information that had been backed up, according to plan at closing time on Friday. Early Monday morning, shipments began arriving from vendors who had been notified of the emergency, according to the plan, on Saturday night.

Late Monday afternoon, less than forty-eight hours after the fire, the first shipments left the Florida Seed Company to be delivered to customers the next day! Without the plan in place, Allen says the company would have been out of business for weeks, perhaps months. Fortunately, because they had a plan, and were ready to implement the plan, they were in a position to adapt to the situation, and their customers hardly even noticed a ripple in the service they provided.

Most often, the challenges you face will not be as dramatic as a fire; but, many little challenges can be just as costly. Companies merge, buyers retire, new products emerge, competitors regroup, illness can strike you or your customer, and a million other things affect your relationship with your customers. The burden to adapt always rests with the seller.

A saw miller named Roy had to adapt to a different challenge. He had a contract to provide utility poles for rural electric co-ops in Georgia, just after World War II. Economic expansion was racing across the country after the war, and utilities were pressed to keep up with the demand for electricity.

Roy was a master track sales pro who saw opportunity in the needs and challenges that faced his customers. With the thought in mind that he could use the same trucks, crews, and equipment that went out into the woods to cut down those tall Georgia pine trees, to go back and stand them up on the right-of-way, he got a contract to build some power lines.

Quickly he had to adapt to a challenge. The companies that sold copper wire in this country at the time were all overloaded with demand. They told Roy it would be eighteen months to two years before they could get him the wire he needed.

Roy said, *"I'll make it myself."*

Many replied, *"You can't do that."*

Roy's response was, *"I'll be caught trying."*

In 1950, Roy Richards and A.A. Case, along with six employees, started making copper wire in Case's backyard in Carrollton, Georgia. Twenty-five years later, that little backyard wire mill had become the largest manufacturer of copper wire in the western world, and the largest supplier of wire making equipment and technology in the entire world.

The companies that could not provide the service Roy needed in 1950 gained a new competitor--and not just any competitor, but a competitor who took the lion's share of the market. Plus, many of those very same companies, each year, pay royalties to the Southwire Corporation for wire making technology developed by Roy Richards, A.A. Case, and the members of the Southwire team.

Adaptability turned a Georgia sawmiller into an international industrial giant. The possibilities are really endless.

Master track sales professionals capitalize on opportunities as they present themselves. You may have a perfect idea, but if the timing is not right, it's best to put it on the back burner and wait. Work on the things the buyer is focused on now, and save the idea for when the time is right. Always adapt your schedule to fit the buyer's timetable.

The need to be adaptable in business is the result of the ever presence of change in the business world. One day it's *downsizing,* the next day it's *right sizing,* and then it's *reengineering.* There will be something else new next month.

One thing that remains constant is the importance of you staying on top of change--change that affects your buyers, trends in the industry, and new strategies by your competition. In business, we wake up to a new world everyday. To get on top and stay on top, you have to be aware of the changes as soon as possible, and react appropriately as soon as possible. You must realize that sales opportunities follow all changes and be eager to adapt.

Top selling professionals learn to adapt using two key skills: *negotiating,* and the *art of compromise.* In any given business situation, the buyer and the seller cannot both get everything they want. Considering just price alone, a trading point has to be established somewhere between *free* and a billion bucks. Sales professionals learn to negotiate a compromise that allows both sides to get what will work for them in terms of price, delivery, and other key points.

85

How to Adapt
to
Difficult Challenges

1) List your worse fears now.

2) Develop a plan to deal with them if they become reality.

3) Remember, long term goals eliminate short term bumps in the road.

4) Keep a firm finger on the pulse of your industry--read the trade magazines, and nurture and maintain good lines of communications with a network of friends in the business

Change is inevitable--progress is not. Master track salespeople are able to adapt and make progress. Average salespeople are more interested in activity rather than achievement. Master track sales pros understand that things work out best for those who make the best of the way things work out.

Bear Traps to Avoid

▶ *Do not focus on the things that could go wrong, ninty per cent of them never do. Always be prepared with a good Plan B. Never focus on the negative.*

▶ *Ignore the colleagues who complain about how the changes will affect them, focus on the customer's needs.*

▶ *Do not change just for the sake of change.*

Selling in the Bear Woods

"Thinking is the hardest work there is,
which is the probable reason why so few engage in it."

-HENRY FORD

THE NINTH DISCIPLINE

Creativity. Be audacious. Practice a little showmanship. Remember the first rule of Vaudeville:

"If you want to make a living, you've got to put on a good show."

A very successful woman we know always wears a hat. Everyone in her industry knows her. They know her by the hats.

You do not have to wear a hat. You should not take this idea to the extreme, as any good idea taken to the extreme becomes a bad idea (as per our *Theory of the A Sharp--You can fine tune an A sharp until it becomes a B flat)*. In fact, too much *dress for success* is over dress in sales. While you should always look professional and presentable, overdressing your clients can make them feel uncomfortable around you.

There are a lot of ways to be creative, and, it's always a good thing to be known for your creativity, especially when your creativity manifests itself in areas of interest to your clients. In any industry, there are legends. The legends became bigger than life because of their creativity.

[Billy Bob Says- *"Ultimately, success in selling comes from creativity."*]

Master track sales professional Julius Talton came up with a creative way to solve a difficult sales problem. A small town Alabama radio station had just acquired the rights to carry Alabama Crimson Tide football. This was not a problem. Advertising during broadcast coverage of Crimson Tide football games in Alabama is a very easy sell.

To get the football games, the station had to agree to carry all of the University's basketball games as well. So, the station was locked into having to move a very difficult inventory of ad time during the winter months, (not good times in the radio business).

Injecting a dose of creativity into the situation, Julius devised a plan to package both sports together. With a buy, an advertiser would get ad time on every Alabama football and basketball game of the season. By offering the package in August, just before football season, buyer's were approached when the high demand football time was the primary focus. With levelized billing over the course of both the football and basketball seasons, (from September through March), the package was priced in such a way as to appeal to buyers with added value while giving the station more revenue than ever for the football broadcasts, and a bonus of great revenue through the slow winter months.

Great sales pros in all industries have learned, creativity, above all, is the best route around price objections. Joel Alderman says, *"It's never the money."* Joel maintains only the government really buys from the low bidder, and he's a proponent of the philosophy that a high bid presented with creativity always gets attention, and attention leads to opportunity.

Sales Champions have "creative peripheral vision"-- more than the ability to see something as it is, but as it could be.

Vidalia Onions are known the world over as premium onions; but what does a farmer do with the ones that turn out less than perfect? Delbert Bland has that *creative peripheral vision.* He saw them as they could be. He buys all the seconds from other onion growers and utilizes them in processed items. Now Bland Farms controls about half of all the Vidalia Onion business in the world.

One young radio salesman we knew used a big dose of creativity to make a difficult sale. The merchant's association in a small town within his station's coverage area had invited him, along with representatives from two other stations, to bid on a remote broadcast during the town's sidewalk sale. He knew the other two would cut the price to get the order. He, on the other hand, did not want just an order, he wanted some real business. Master track sales people know the difference. It's numerical and includes commas and decimal points.

Through planning and preparation, this young man arranged to be the last station rep to present at the meeting. The first salesman offered a deal that represented a sizable cut in his normal rate structure. The second presenter got out a pitching wedge and cut under the first.

Then, the savvy young sales pro made his offer. His station would do the remote free for the association, provided at least twenty of the members would buy a minimum schedule of advertising from his station at normal rates during the week of the sidewalk sale. He got the deal, and the decimal points.

Later in life he reflected, *"The highest compliment I have ever been paid by a competitor came as a result of that sale, the sales manager from one of the other stations said I robbed Childersburg!"*

In another situation, his station was in the position of being on the outside looking in. His market was Talladega, Alabama, home of NASCAR's Winston 500. The other station in town had the rights to broadcast the races. Each season, during race week, he sat on his hands and watched them make big dollars off pre-race festivities and the race itself.

Creativity leads to solutions when you live in the *Land of Make-Do*. He decided to compete with NASCAR and promote his own race.

[Billy Bob Says- *"Never be a 'me too' salesman when you can use creativity to come up with something better, like 'me/2', because it's better to be different than to lose your identity trying to be better."***]**

Successful radio entrepreneurs are known for their creativity. Here's the story our friend relayed to us about how his station used creativity to overcome the problem.

Since we didn't have a speedway and didn't know any race car owners, we decided to promote the world's first sanctioned watermelon race! The police said some 2,000 people attended the first Watermelon 500. Our radio station was the sanctioning body so we drew up the rules. Kids raced watermelons around a track we drew off with marble dust in a field next to the Chevy Dealer who sponsored the promotion. If a kid busted his watermelon, our Grand Marshall ruled him out of competition due to a "blown engine." Several hundred kids raced in the Watermelon 500. They all got T-shirts, the

Chevy dealer sold cars, and we did business! Our conservative estimates indicated we did about twice as much business off the Watermelon 500 as our competitor did with the Winston 500.

In a similar promotion, we bought a junk car for $600 and turned it into $50,000 profit before we gave it away six months later. The idea came as a result of brain storming to find a way to compete with another station that was giving away two brand new cars. They spent more, we made more!

[Billy Bob Says- *"Bear selling pros must get outside the box, doing what others are not willing or able to do...and they must also get the buyers outside the box so they can both grow.]*

Creativity is the magic you can use to maximize sales efforts and parlay profits. Master track sales people use generous doses of creativity when selling in the bear woods.

Ways to Juice Up
Your Creativity

▶ *Always ask, how can we be different?*

▶ *Study the successes in other industries and emulate their creativity.*

▶ *Find ways to create an environment where your customer wants to do business with you, and look for ways to make it easy for your customers to do business with you.*

▶ *Customize, customize, customize! Make the presentation fit the situation and always make everything you do account specific.*

▶ *Remember, different is always better than just better.*

Bear Traps to Avoid

1) Developing ideas or items that lose sight of the need the buyer wants filled.

2) Loading up the idea with too many bells and whistles, allowing the creativity to upstage the product.

3) Losing sight of the goal of making it easy for the customer to business with you.

*"It makes great difference in the force of a sentence
whether a man be behind it or not."*

-EMERSON

THE TENTH DISCIPLINE

Communication. Now it's time for you to talk. While a text book study would define communication as a two way street, we have separated the two areas of listening and talking. It is no accident that listening came first in this book. It's a higher discipline. After you have listened and ascertained your prospects' needs, the time will come for you to express yourself. It's still a two way street; but, at this point, at least it's time for you to make your presentation.

An individual who can express him or herself well before groups of people, and in one on one situations, is perceived as intelligent and as one who should be listened to, even if they know nothing and have nothing of value to say.

[Billy Bob Says- *"Those who have grand ideas and cannot express them to others, are no better off than those who never have any ideas at all."***]**

Selling does not happen without communication. Master track sales professionals are masterful communicators. They know how to write letters that stir action. They know how to create and present presentations that rivet attention, arouse curiosity, and bring buyers to the point of close. More over, they know how to get right to the heart of the matter, one on one, with master track buyers who expect more and demand more.

Questions That Must Be Answered

1) Why do you do business with me?

2) Am I bringing value in the products and pricing?

When communicating with customers and prospects,

always have a plan. Plan what you should do before the call. Know what you want to accomplish during the call and keep your goal in focus. Plan for follow up after the call. Doing the right things at the right times speaks volumes to your customers as *actions* really do *speak louder than words.*

Improving your communication skills will help you sell more effectively. You will be tempted to identify your weak areas and work on them first (good idea); but, do not forget to campaign your strength.

As with everything else in the bear woods, go back to the basics and pay attention to all the little details. Consider the following comments from a master track sales professional.

> *Understand the importance of staying in touch. I've had salespeople who had no sense of urgency in returning phone calls. Not only do you miss many opportunities, but also tend to hack the buyer off if phone calls are not returned immediately. The buyer's perception is "they must not need the business" if calls are not returned within a reasonable amount of time. Even if you have negative information, or cannot do the deal, call back promptly and let them know. Many times the buyer will ask, "Well, what can you do?" This opens the door for opportunity and negotiation.*

If you are fairly strong communicating one on one, but feel you could use improvement speaking before groups, work on both. In the natural progression of life, things that are not growing wither and die.

We also suggest you study the masters, not the professors. Read the works of great communicators from the fields of advertising, sales and politics; and, listen to the masters from the arena of public speaking. Unlike the professors who know the theory but have little practical experience, master communicators, such as, Martin Luther King, David Ogilivy, Og Mandino, Cavett Robert, Rosita Perez, Sir Winston Churchill, John Caples, Dr. Norman Vincent Peale, and hundreds more, have mastered the art of communications in the arena of practical application with tremendous, measurable, success. You can hear, and see, and study their works, and in most cases, read in their own words how they achieved mastery.

While you do not have to become a grand orator, your growth in sales will rest on your ability to continually improve your communication skills. Great writers and speakers have a way with words. Economist have a way with numbers. Great sales professionals have a way with both.

How to Improve
Your Communications Skills

▶ *Never write a letter or presentation once. Start with a rough draft like you did in school.*

▶ *Practice all spoken presentations until you have mastered them before you present them. Have a co-worker challenge your presentation and play devil's advocate.*

▶ *Learn from the masters, study the great ones.*

▶ *Touch base with those who haven't called, return the calls of those you have missed.*

▶ *Be consistent, don't be labeled as one who never calls unless he wants something.*

▶ *Always get back to your prospects and customers promptly.*

Bear Traps to Avoid

1) Never become a commercial visitor by calling, or calling on, a buyer just to chat.

2) Avoid failing to clearly answer all questions raised by the buyer. Leaving questions unanswered leads buyers to question your ability.

3) Avoid the use of industry jargon that your customers and prospects do not understand.

4) Remember the importance of clearly communicating benefits over features.

"For they conquer who believe they can."

-Virgil

THE ELEVENTH DISCIPLINE

Optimism. You have got to be a card toting, orthodox, died in the wool, genuine, deeply devout, born again optimist, who is convinced everything is perfect and going to get even better. If your pony died, you'd see it as an opportunity to sell glue.

Your enthusiastic case of optimism should be so potent and contagious you are identified as a carrier and all who come in contact with you are affected by it. Indeed, they even feel better for just having been around you.

[Billy Bob Says- *"People who can get other people excited about ideas and opportunities shall inherit the very best accounts on earth."*]

How do you turn up your level of optimism? The process is very simple. Hang out with optimistic people. Attitudes are highly contagious. As we travel though this adventure we call life, we have a way of arriving at a common destination with our traveling companions. That's why your momma told you to choose the right friends. It's why your grandma used to remind you that *birds of a feather flock together.* It's also why King Solomon said, *"He that walketh with wise men shall be wise."*

So, to improve you level of optimism, stay away from down-in-the-mouth deadbeats and hang out with optimistic people who are going places. Become one who celebrates life and sees opportunity around every corner.

People who have negative attitudes are not in sales-- they are in sales prevention.

A good cheerful attitude is essential in master track

selling. People like to do business with optimistic, enthusiastic people. Plus, optimistic salespeople are encouragers to the buyers they deal with, they lift their buyers up and help them to grow. BONUS: as your customers grow, you grow.

Optimistic salespeople can be challenging and more aggressive without alienating the buyer. Buyers expect optimistic salespeople to tell them, *"No is an unacceptable answer."* Buyers also tend to turn to their most optimistic vendors for help when it comes to solving their most challenging problems. This leads to more decimal points.

"Enthusiasm is the flywheel which will carry your saw through the knots in the log."

-Dr. Harold Cushing

Optimistic people are excited about what they do. They have a way of powering through adversity, difficulty, and the many challenges of today's world of business. They are the kind of people master track buyers seek out as partners when looking for reliable vendors to help them solve their problems and meet their needs.

*"The greater the difficulty,
the more glory in surmounting it."*
-EPICURUS

Spread Your Optimism

Dr. Charles Petty knows how to spread optimism and good cheer. When traveling on holidays, he makes a point of walking up to airline employees and saying, *"I just want you to know how much I appreciate you working today so I can get where I need to go."* Nobody likes to work on holidays, but Charles makes them feel good anyway. That's what optimists do, they make others feel good in spite of the situation.

Developing Your Spirit of Optimism

▶ *Learn to highlight and repeat only the good news.*

▶ *Refuse to be surprised by trouble, or troubled by negative thoughts.*

▶ *Use your imagination to visualize your success in all situations.*

▶ *Learn to accept what you cannot change.*

▶ *Be of good cheer, even when you aren't happy.*

▶ *Practice saying things to others that will make them feel good.*

"Well done, thou good and faithful servant: thou has been faithful over a few things, I will make thee ruler over many things."

MATTHEW 25:2 I

THE FINAL DISCIPLINE

Service. This is the fuel that drives the free enterprise system. In this economy, everone who is paid, is paid to do something for someone else. You earn your livelihood by providing service for your fellowman. That is the only way to turn a profit in the free enterprise system.

[**Billy Bob Says-** *"There is a direct correlation between good service and good sales."*]

    The free enterprise system was introduced in the New World when Captain John Smith said, *"If you don't work, you don't eat."* To work means to provide something of value for someone else. Profit occurs when the value to the customer is greater than what it cost you to provide it.

    Maybe you sell products. A product is the noun version of the verb *service*. A product's value is determined by what it will do for people, and the word *do* indicates action, so the verb tense of *product* is *service*. (An English teacher may not see it this way, but what do English teachers know about selling?)

    Consequently, everyone in the free enterprise system has customers. Doctors call them patients, lawyers call them clients, politicians call them constituents, and English teachers call them students (although most English teachers do not understand the concept of selling, if they did, they would have sold us on the idea of learning more when we were in school).

    Paul Blazer, the founder of Ashland Oil Company, said, *"Ours is not a world of things, it is a world of people."* Mr. Blazer was right. Selling is nothing more and nothing less than helping people find and get the things they want or need. To do this, you have to earn the trust and respect of the people you want to serve.

    Jeanne Primeux mastered the craft in a unique way. She was the first woman inducted into the *President's Service*

Club by Cook's Pest Control. In fact, her supervisor had challenged her by saying, *"Jeanne, no woman has ever been inducted into the President's Service Club."*

To Jeanne, those were fighting words. A year later, the president of the company, Mr. Cook, stood before the group at the annual induction banquet and called her name.

As Jeanne approached the podium to receive her recognition, Mr. Cook raised his hand and said, *"Before I give this to Jeanne, there's a story I've just got to tell you about her."* He went on to relate the following story.

Jeanne had arrived at the hotel that afternoon. When she opened the door to her hotel room, there was a dozen long stemmed red roses on the table in the room. At first, she thought maybe they had been sent by her supervisor, but then she thought maybe they were sent by the president of the company. When Jeanne opened the envelope and looked at the card, she learned, the roses had been sent by *ten of her customers*, back home in Memphis, Tennessee!

After the banquet that night, while she was being congratulated by friends and colleagues, someone asked, *"Jeanne, how do you get your customers to send you flowers?"*

"Oh," Jeanne blushed, *"I don't really think of them as customers, I think of them as friends."*

Jeanne's supervisor was standing nearby and he said, *"Jeanne's right, she doesn't really have customers, she has friends. Why, she know's them all on a first name basis, and she knows their birthdays, and she never forgets their birthdays. She even knows their kids names, and their kids birthdays, and she never ever forgets the kid's birthdays!"*

Then the supervisor went on to say, *"You're really not going to believe this, but Jeanne even knows their pets by name, and she takes little treats to their pets."*

Perhaps you know, the two most common concerns shared by consumers when they call a pest control company are: 1) the welfare of their children, and 2) the welfare of their pets. You don't have to worry when you call Jeanne. You know she cares. Her customers know, not because she tells them, but because she *shows them*!

Minor league sales people try to tell their customers they care. Master track sales people show their customers they care.

Jeanne Primeaux was sixty-two years old when she took a job as a pest control technician. She had already retired from a successful career with secure retirement benefits. Jeanne didn't get in it for the money, she got in it for the flowers.

Upper level sales professionals always go after the flowers. That's why they never have to worry about the money.

[Billy Bob Says- *"Your customers are those who benefit from whatever it is you do when you say you are working."*]

&

[Billy Bob Also Says- *"Customer service is making it easy for your*

customers to do business with you."]

Based on Billy Bob's principle above, here is a hard saying that you must fully understand as a rite of passage into the bear woods of big league selling:

The primary benefactor of the sell should always be the buyer!

Write it on the rock. When you believe it, and learn how to always make it happen, you will be a master of the art and worthy of the title: *High Champion, Black Belt, Top Spot, Bear Woods, Master Track Sales Professional.* Your friends, however, will be more impressed with the numerical results, the ones with commas and decimal points. Your banker will probably start asking you for advice.

From Bryan Townsend's customer service seminar, *The Only Job Description You Will Ever Need,* here is a true life success story of one who made it happen.

A small town bank asked me to speak at their annual customer appreciation banquet. I had never heard of such an event. The bank I use puts a little sign in the lobby that reads-"we appreciate your business". Sometimes, they stick a little notice in my check statement that says, "we appreciate your business"; sometimes they stick one in that says, "We'd appreciate it more if you'd stop by and make a deposit!"

But, this little bank likes to show their customers that they care, so each year, they host an annual customer appreciation banquet and they invite several hundred of their best customers. One year, they invited me to be the speaker.

When I arrived at the civic center, rather early, only one person was there. An older man whom I assumed was a retired gentleman in the community who had taken on the responsibility of looking after the little country civic center, which used to be the National Guard Armory.

But, shortly after I arrived, a truck pulled up out back and this gentlemen went out to help bring in the food. At this point I assumed he was the caterer, there to cater the banquet.

When guests started arriving, the older gentleman stationed himself at the front door and began to welcome the guests. He was shaking hands, patting people on the back, and thanking them for coming.

During dinner, the old fellow was busy moving around the hall. He was waiting on people, serving tea and coffee, and fetching anything anyone needed. I leaned over to Sylvia Middlebrooks, the vice president of the bank, seated next to me at the head table, and asked her: "Who is this gentleman out here who has been so busy waiting on people tonight?"

"Oh," she said, "that's Mr. Faulkner, he's my boss, he owns this bank!"

When the banquet ended, Mr. Faulkner was up waiting on people. He was shaking hands, thanking people for coming, and telling them how much he appreciated their business.

Then, as the last guests left, Mr. Faulkner took off his jacket, loosened his tie, grabbed a trash can, and started to drag it around the hall, cleaning off the tables. I'm no dummy, I took off my jacket, rolled up my sleeves, and started to help Mr. Faulkner.

Late that night, out back of the civic center, as Mr. Faulkner and I were dumping the last load of trash into the dumpster, I turned to him and asked; "Mr. Faulkner, all of this I have seen you do here tonight, is all of this in your job description?"

He looked at me for just a moment, and then replied, "Young man, I only have one job description, and that is to satisfy my customers."

That's really the only job description any of us will ever need, it's the only mission statement any company ever really needs. You always satisfy the customer, and who knows, you might even wind up owning the bank!

In this story, it's obvious Mr. Faulkner understands the primary benefactor of the sell should always be the buyer. Your typical used car salesman does not realize this, but, he doesn't own the bank. However, to get to the next level in sales, it is a principle he will have to learn.

Selling, at the highest level, is finding and delivering goods and services needed by your customers. Often, a customer does not know a particular good or service is needed, or available. The sales professional, in the spirit of service, identifies a need or a use, comes up with an idea to solve a problem, and communicates the idea in such a way that helps the buyer to understand, and when the dust settles, the buyer is better off for it. So, the buyer turns to the seller for help on a regular basis, and sooner or later the seller may sit on the board at the bank!

All Customers Want the Same Thing

It's the very same thing you want when you spend your money--*Value*. V*alue* is the work product of the seller. It is your job to deliver value to the marketplace.

V*alue* is always in the eye of the beholder, the buyer. Buyers set the standards. They determine what to buy, when to buy, where to buy, and how much to buy. All of these decisions are based on their perceptions, not yours. Consequently, the buyer's opinion is the only one that counts.

Regardless of how much value you place on an item, real value is what it will bring--the price real buyers are willing to pay. The same thing goes for service. The buyer's opinion is the only one that counts. If it's a problem for the buyer, your partner, it's a problem for you. If it's good for the buyer, it's good for you.

Mythology has it that people buy from their friends. This is true, only when buyers can depend on their friends for value. Long term friendship ends when a buyer feels shafted.

Like the knights of old who swore allegiance to the King, master track sales professionals are valiant servants who serve their buyers. They understand the wisdom in the ancient philosophy:

When you go about your daily routine
with the attitude of a servant,
the people you serve, will crown you King!

Welcome to the bear woods. Good luck & good hunting!

Suggestions
for
Insuring Service

▶ *Constantly review procedures and policies to make sure it's easy for your customers to do business with you.*

▶ *Always deliver on time, or sooner.*

▶ *Remember the customer's opinion is the only one that counts, so judge service by their standards, not yours.*

Service Bear Traps to Avoid

▶ *Without guidance, your people will search for ways to make it easier for them to do their jobs, with disregard for the needs of your customers. This can make it difficult for customers to do business with you and quite often is the reason buyers look for new vendors.*

▶ *Assuming that all customers are interested only in obtaining the lowest price and service is not a factor.**

* *At this moment, are you wearing the cheapest shoes you could have bought, driving the cheapest car you could have bought, and living in the cheapest home or apartment you could have found? No? You look for value when you spend your money. So do your customers. Value is the work product of service.*

*"It is a socialist idea that making profits is vice.
I consider the real vice is making losses."*

-WINSTON CHURCHILL

IN CONCLUSION

Most master track sales professionals are:

easy to work with, comfortable to be around, mild mannered,

moderately dressed, soft spoken, and honest to a fault.

This is not the image you get when you see a *salesman* portrayed on TV, and it's not what most people think of when they hear the term, *high powered salesman.*

Yet, the sales champions we have known and have consulted for this work were all: top professionals (in the fields of automotive sales, food sales, time sales, insurance sales, equipment sales, and the sales of industrial supplies); and they were comfortable to be around, mild mannered, moderately dressed, soft spoken, and honest to a fault. In sales, competition is stiff, buyers are demanding, and it's almost impossible to get to the top without being all of these and mastering all of the disciplines described in this book.

First it takes desire. If you have the desire, through time on task, work will get you where you want to go. Like a master musician who learns all the chords, or a golf pro who masters all the clubs, invest time wisely to master the disciplines and link them together as a master mason applies the mortar to the brick to build a firm foundation. Good luck with your quest!

Selling in the Bear Woods

When I first started selling,
I didn't know if I could;
But with practice and encouragement,
I got pretty good.

Then I decided to study and work,
leaving nothing to fate.
I found that's what it takes,
if you want to be great.

If you are tired of chasing rabbits,
just do the things you know you should.
Soon you'll find yourself selling
in the Bear Woods!

-Bryan Townsend

Billy Bob's Suggested Reading List:

Credibility:
 The Greatest Salesman in the World by Og Mandino

Empathy:
See You at the Top by Zig Ziglar

Listening:
Effective Listening-- Key to Your Success by Lyman K. Steil, Larry L. Barker & Kittie Watson

Personality:
Personality Plus by Florence Littauer

Knowledge:
Mission Possible by Og Mandino

Drive:
Life is Tremendous By Charles "T" Jones
Bear by Paul W. Bryant & John Underwood

Confidence:
The Confidence Factor by Alan Loy McGinnis

Adaptability:
The Goal by Eliyahu M. Goldratt & Jeff Cox

Creativity:
Confessions of An Advertising Man by David Ogilvy

Communications:
Bringing Out the Best in People by Alan Loy McGinnis
How to Make Your Advertising Make Money by John Caples

Optimism:
The Power of Positive Thinking by Norman Vincent Peale
The Power of Optimism by Alan Loy McGinnis

Service:
Service America by Karl Albrecht & Ron Zemke
It's Not My Department by Peter Glen

Share Your Success

Let us know about your most exciting achievements in the sales profession. We'd like to know how you have used one of the disciplines listed in the book, or some other technique, to accomplish a major sales goal. Plus, we'd love to hear your ideas about growing in sales. What have you done that has worked for you?

Write to us at either of the addresses listed on the next page. Tell us what you have accomplished and how you did it. Include your name, address, and telephone number, along with your E-mail address. Also, if you would be so kind, include permission for us to use your submission in a future book. If our editors select your submission, you'll receive a complimentary autographed copy when the book is published.

To Contact the Authors:

Both Bob Mann & Bryan Townsend are professional speakers who are available for keynote & seminar presentations. For information regarding availability, or for information about their motivational tapes, you can reach them as follows:

Bob Mann
P.O. Box 381165
Duncanville, TX 75138

Bryan Townsend, CSP
P.O. Box 994
Talladega, AL 35161

Certified
Master Track
Bear Selling
Professional

You are now entitled to receive a certificate acknowledging your completion of this book and your work to master the twelve disciplines of Selling in the Bear Woods.

To receive your certificate, suitable for framing, send your name and address to:

Bryan Townsend
P.O. Box 994
Talladega, AL 35161